KNOWING HOLY SPIRIT

Chelsea Kong

Printed in 2021, Made in Toronto, Canada
ISBN: 978-1-990399-07-7
Library and Archives Canada

Be close to the Holy Spirit and you will not be alone.

Just to say thanks, you can get free books.
Email: kayunkk@gmail.com

Trust the Holy Spirit.

He is always with us.

He knows everything.

WHO IS THE HOLY SPIRIT?

He is equal to God, He is God's Spirit

He works with Him and lets us hear God.

He was there since the beginning and He works in us.

He created the earth with God (Genesis 1:2).

HOLY SPIRIT IN GOD'S WORD

He has many names in the Bible.

Many times, Holy Spirit is not clearly seen in the Bible.

He is always working with every person.

He works on the outside and the inside of us.

Holy Spirit knows all things.

He understands.

He guides us.

He gives us power and teaches us to fear God.
(Isaiah 11:2 ICB)

HOLY SPIRIT

He comes as a dove, light, wind, breath, and more.

He came upon Jesus as a dove when he was baptized.

Holy Spirit helps us in our weaknesses.

Holy Spirit will live inside us when we have Jesus.

HOLY SPIRIT COMES

He is the Spirit of Truth that helps us know God's Word.

He tells us about Jesus and you can tell Him anything.

Holy Spirit helps us in our weaknesses.

Holy Spirit will live inside us when we have Jesus.

HOLY SPIRIT

He is the Spirit of Truth that
helps us know God's Word.

He tells us about Jesus and
you can tell Him anything.

Holy Spirit is patient, kind, and doesn't like sin.

He will rest on those who follow Jesus.

Holy Spirit prays

Holy Spirit gives us languages.

He can speak through us in tongues from heaven.

He can speak in the language on earth.

He gives us the words to pray and prays through us.

ADEUS

CIAO

SHALOM

AU REVOIR

FARVEL

ZAI JIAN

GOOD BYE

He gives us love, joy, peace.

Patience, kindness, goodness, faithfulness.

FRUIT OF THE HOLY SPIRIT

Gentleness, and self-control. (Galatians 5:22-23)

We become like Jesus when we grow in these.

HIS GIFTS

- Spirit of wisdom
- Knowledge
- Faith
- Healing
- Miracles

- Prophesy
- Difference between good and evil spirits.
- Different kinds of languages.
- Ability to interpret languages.

Office Gifts

💗 **Apostle to build His Church.**

💗 **Prophet to tell us about the future.**

💗 **Evangelist to lead us to have Jesus.**

💗 **Pastor to share God's love.**

💗 **Teacher to teach us God's Word.**

GIFT OF TONGUES

This is to speak in another language.

It can be a language from our world.

It can the language from heaven.

Holy Spirit makes our tongue
speak it when we open our mouth.

GIFT OF KNOWLEDGE

Holy Spirit tells us things about the past and now.

He will let you know about a problem.

GIFT OF WISDOM

Holy Spirit will tell you what to do.

He will give you the words and it helps others.

People need to follow what He says.

It is something we did not know.

GIFT OF FAITH

Holy Spirit gives us His faith to believe.

This faith can help people to be free or healed.

You know what you believe will happen.

It is unlimited faith.

GIFT OF MIRACLES

Holy Spirit gives us the ability to do miracles.

This gift can make something unseen become real.

This gift brings dead people to life.

It can multiple things that we need.

GIFT OF HEALING

Holy Spirit can heal our body, mind, and soul.

It can be a miracle healing.

The healing can happen right away or takes time.

You know when somebody will be healed.

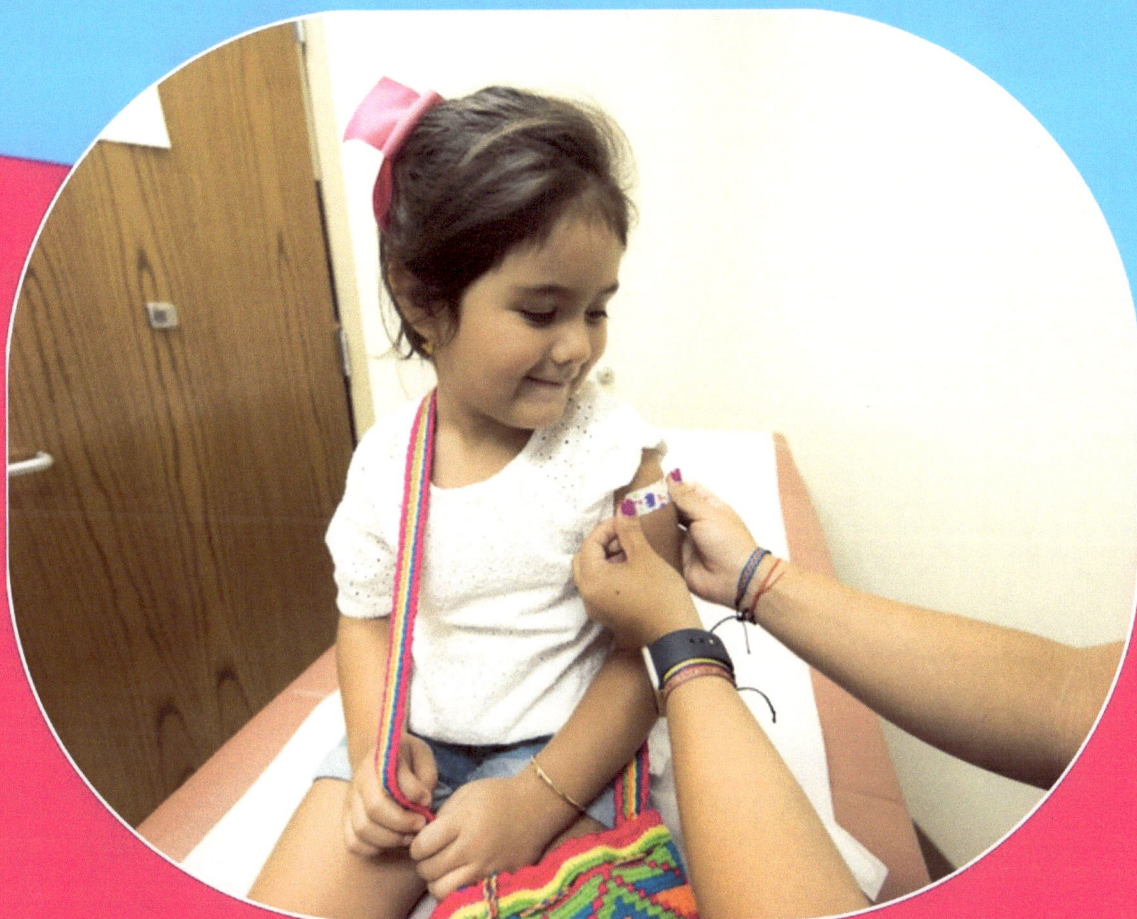

GIFT OF PROPHECY

Holy Spirit speaks through us about the future.

He will let us know our future and other people's.

It should give strength,
encourage, and comfort.

You must speak with love
when you prophesy.

DIFFERENCE OF SPIRITS

He knows when there is a good spirit or bad spirit.

You will know their name.

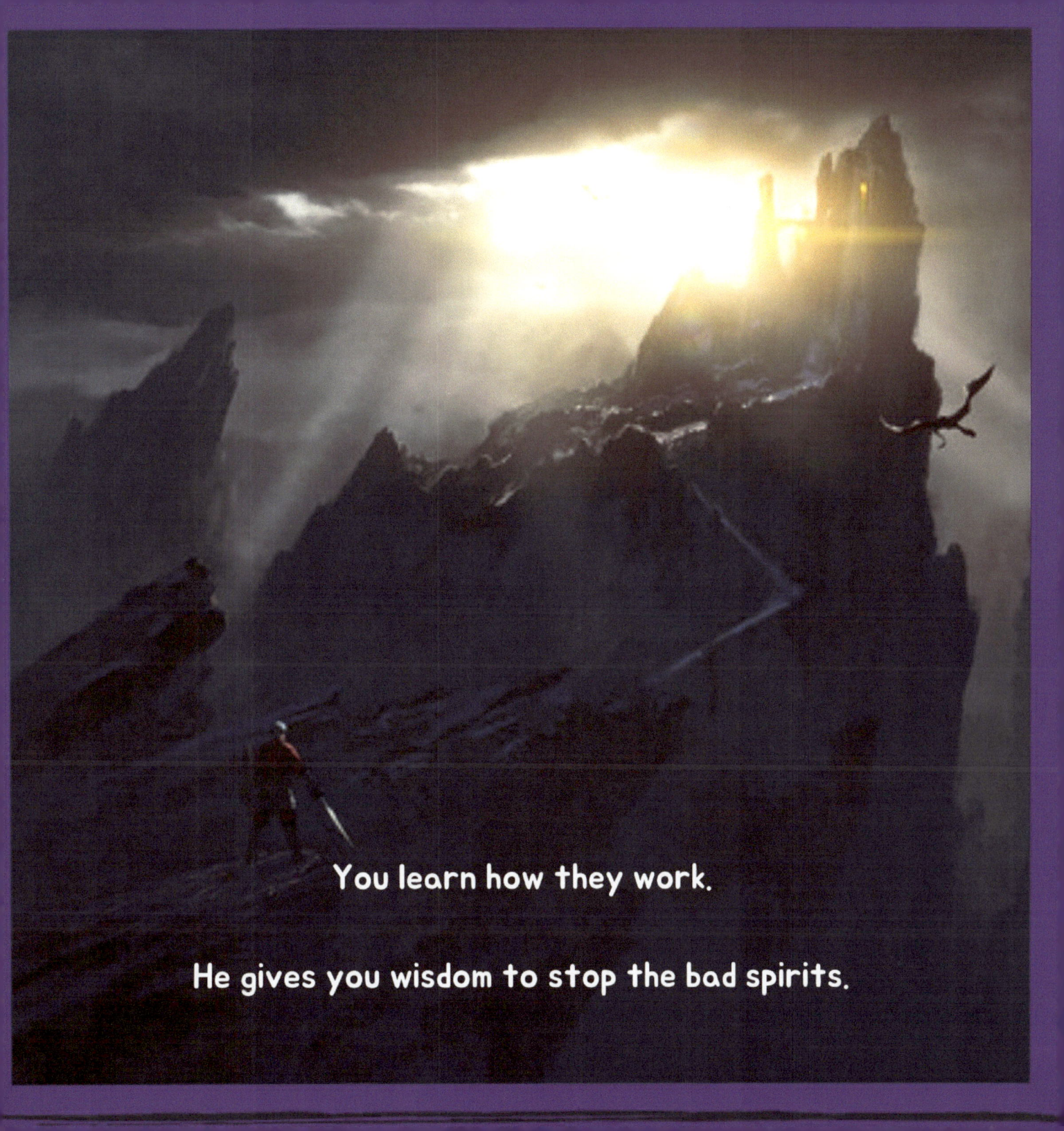

You learn how they work.

He gives you wisdom to stop the bad spirits.

DIFFERENT KINDS OF LANGUAGES

You can speak different languages.

Holy Spirit tells you what to say in the language.

Holy Spirit gives you the
gift to learn it.

You know which language
people speak.

ABILITY TO INTERPRET LANGUAGES

You know how to translate the language well.

You understand what they mean.

Holy Spirit tells you what it means.

You can understand many languages.

GIFTS IN THE BIBLE

Administration

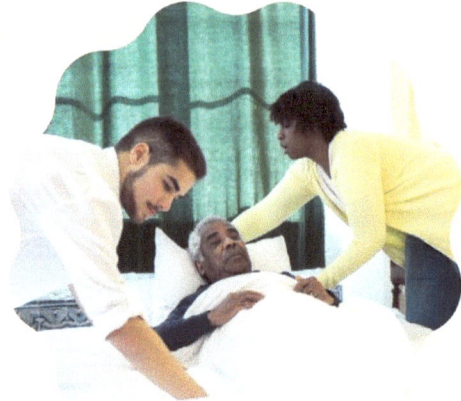

Helps

Serving

Teaching

(Romans 12:6-7)

Encourage

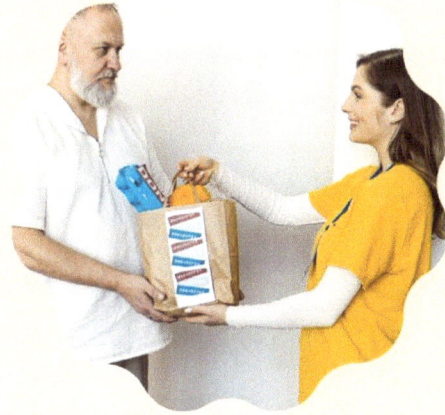

Giving to others

Being a Leader

Being Kind to others

(Romans 12:8)

HOLY SPIRIT IN US

Holy Spirit makes us clean for God.

He gives us power and anointing to do God's work.

He reminds us of God's Word.

He works in our heart to
change us and restore us.

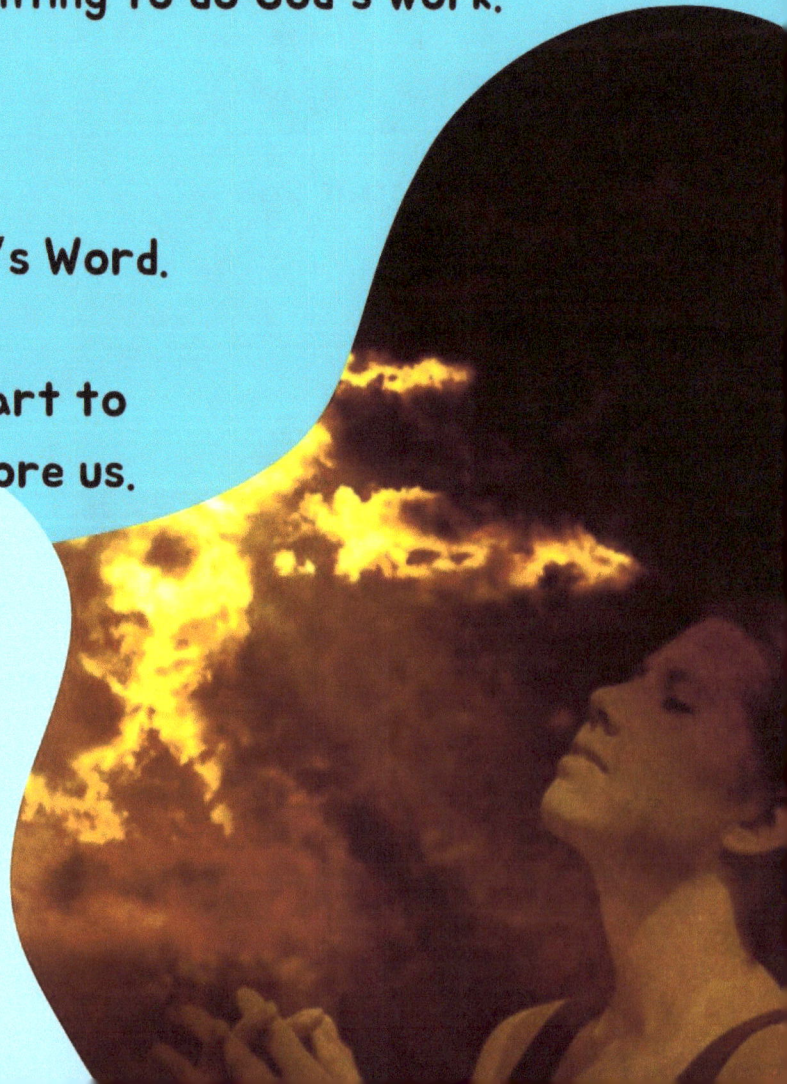

MORE ABOUT HIM

Holy Spirit loves to sing songs to us.

He can help us to pray all the time.

He stops the evil one from destroying God's people.

Holy Spirit came upon David and Jesus' disciples.

OTHER ROLES

Holy Spirit protects us from danger.

He brings us close to God and Jesus.

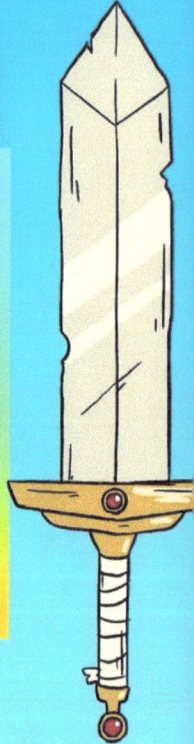

He helps us enter into God's Presence and Glory.

He makes us strong in the Lord and helps us to fight the devil.

BAPTISM OF WATER

Holy Spirit is with us.

We show people that we believe in Him.

This means we have a new life.

We need to pray and read God's word to grow in Him.

BAPTISM OF THE HOLY SPIRIT

Holy Spirit makes us strong and works inside us.

He makes us aware of God and need Him.

We are able to pray better and more.

He gives us love for God more and worship Him more.

BAPTISM OF FIRE

It makes you hate sin and become pure as gold.

It kills our flesh and makes us become like Jesus.

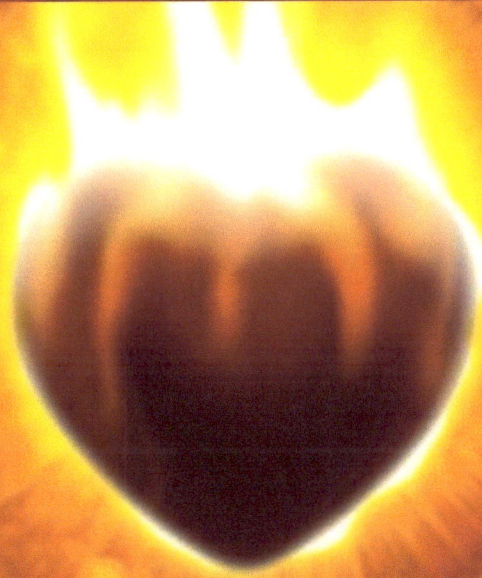

We are totally changed.

It is a test of faith to go through pain.

FINAL WORDS

He gives dreams, visions, and the prophetic.

On the day of Pentecost, He gave the gift of tongues.

Holy Spirit will take the church to heaven.

He will come like fire to judge the earth.

SALVATION PRAYER

God, I know I sinned against you. Forgive me for the wrong that I have done. I believe that Jesus Christ died on the cross for me. That He rose from the grave so that after three days. I can have His long-lasting life. Come into my heart to be my Lord and Savior. I choose to turn away from my sins and I choose to follow you. Lead me to walk with you. Keep me safe and teach me your ways. Stop every bad thing in my life that has an open door to hurt me. Close those doors. Holy Spirit fill me now in Jesus' name. Amen.

BAPTISM IN THE HOLY SPIRIT

Jesus, you are the one that fills me with Your Spirit. Come Holy Spirit and come into my life and fill me to overflow with Your presence. Come with your fire too. Thank you for the gift of tongues in Jesus' name. Amen.

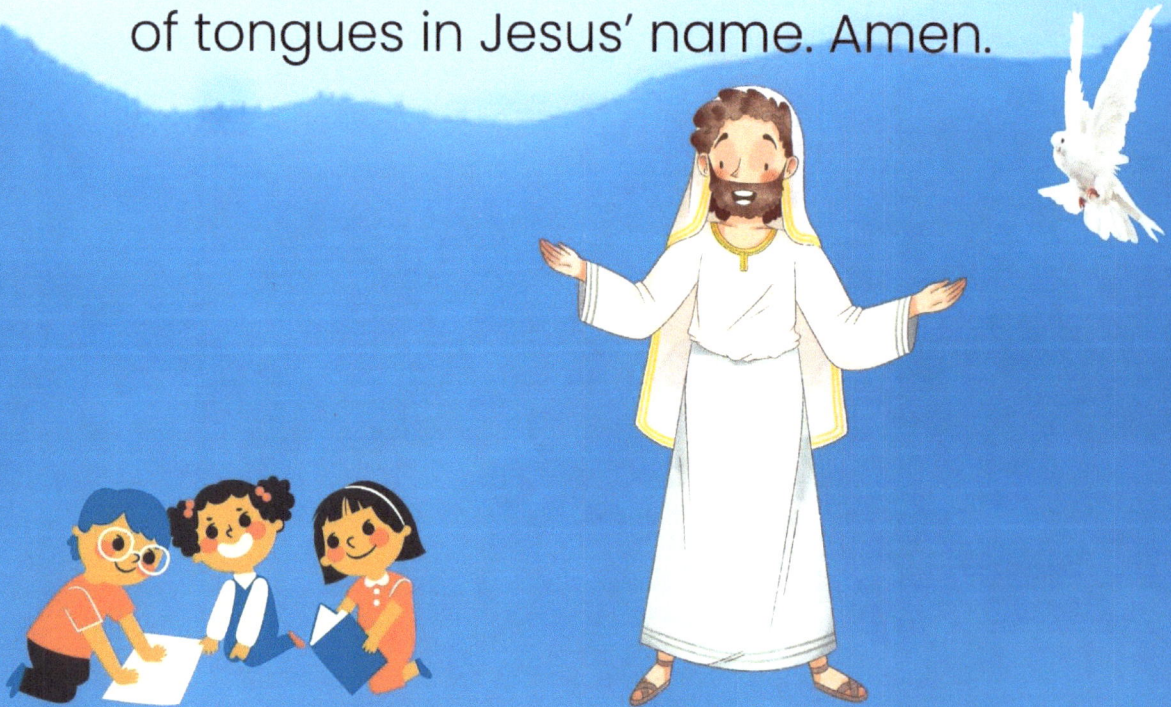

Open your mouth and let the words come out that God gives you. It will be words that you don't know what they mean. You can ask God what it means. You need to let Him talk through you every day to grow this gift.

He will bring you closer to God and you will know Jesus more. You will have power from God to do great things and know things.

PRAYER

Thank you, Father, for dreams and visions. I pray that you will give me the meaning to the dreams and visions that you give me. Teach me how to pray over them.

Guide my steps to walk in your ways and your plan safely in Jesus' name. Amen.

Message from the Author

God speaks to us through dreams when He is not able to get us to hear Him when we are awake. Dreams can also give us ideas. Visions cannot be changed because God decides what He wants to do. We can also dream about heaven and hell. God brings people there so that they can share with others. He wants people to know Him. He wants them to have Jesus in their heart and the Holy Spirit to lead them. He wants us to put our trust in Him and tell Him everything. He will tell us what to do.

OTHER PRODUCTS

Knowing God

How to Hear God's Voice

New Life in Jesus

Loving Israel

God's Gifts

Meeting God

Word Power

Fruit of the Spirit

The Tabernacle

Bride for Jesus

A Life of Prayer

Live Free

Who am I in Jesus

Walk in Love

God's Favor

Man of God

Woman of God

How to Use Money

God's Wisdom

Fasting

See Jerusalem and Bethany

First Fruit Offering

Feast of Trumpets

Day of Atonement

Feast of Tabernacles

Counting the Omer

Festival of Lights

Glory, Presence, and Holy Spirit

Live in God's Presence

31 Day Devotional

Biblical Puzzle Book Vol 1

Biblical Puzzle Book Vol 2

Biblical Puzzle Book Vol 3

Biblical Puzzle Book Vol 4

Biblical Puzzle Book Vol 5

Bible Puzzles for Young
Children Book 1

Bible Puzzles for Young
Children Book 2

Bible Puzzles for Young
Children Book 3

Biblical Puzzle for Children Books 1-3

How God Speaks

Knowing Jesus

Knowing Holy Spirit

OTHER PRODUCTS

Teaching Series

How to Hear God's Voice Teaching Guide & Audio Book

Relationship with God, Jesus, Holy

Spirit Guide

Knowing God, Jesus, Holy Spirit Guide & Audio Book

Teaching (Non-Sale)

Purim

Passover

Resurrection

More books to come!

More books on Amazon, Kobo, and Barnes and Noble
https://chelseak532002550.wordpress.com/

More books on Amazon, Kobo, and Barnes and Noble
https://www.amazon.com/author/chelseakong

Please leave a review and share with friends to help the author continue to write more books to reach more readers. Thank you so much for your support.

About
CHELSEA KONG

She is a writer, creative arts and digital media artist, skilled administration professional, and podcaster. Chelsea also served in a variety of roles, from audiovisual, photography, to assisting on the worship team, and ministry team. She also has a passion for families being united.

Chelsea has been a guest on Unity Live Radio and The Lady Tracey Show and is highly recommended by a Proud Christian blog. She graduated from Hotel and Restaurant Management, Digital Media Arts, Office Administration, and experience working with children. Chelsea lives in Toronto, Canada. She mainly writes children's books, stories, bridal writing, poems, lyrics for songs, words of encouragement, blessings, prayers, and jokes. The author of How to Hear the Voice of God, the Bridal Collection, Knowing God, etc. She also has her own Bible Puzzle books and other inspired products. Her podcast channel is called Chelsea K on Anchor, Spotify, and iTunes.

Please check my website to find out more:
https://chelseak532002550.wordpress.com/

www.ingramcontent.com/pod-product-compliance
Lightning Source LLC
LaVergne TN
LVHW072134070426
835513LV00003B/100